Iain MacIvor BA, FSA, FSA Scot
Chief Inspector of Ancient Monuments

HISTORIC  SCOTLAND

EDINBURGH: HMSO

Introduction

A Formidable Stronghold

The first Blackness Castle was built in the 15th century. It was used as a state prison until the 1707 Treaty of Union. Works starting in 1537 transformed the castle into one of the most formidable artillery fortifications in Scotland. Besieged and damaged by Cromwell's army in 1650, a general repair was begun under Charles II. A long period of obscurity as a minor garrison followed the 1707 Treaty of Union, until 1870-74, when Blackness was converted into an ammunition depot. The Office of Works conserved the castle as an ancient monument when it was finally abandoned for military purposes after World War I.

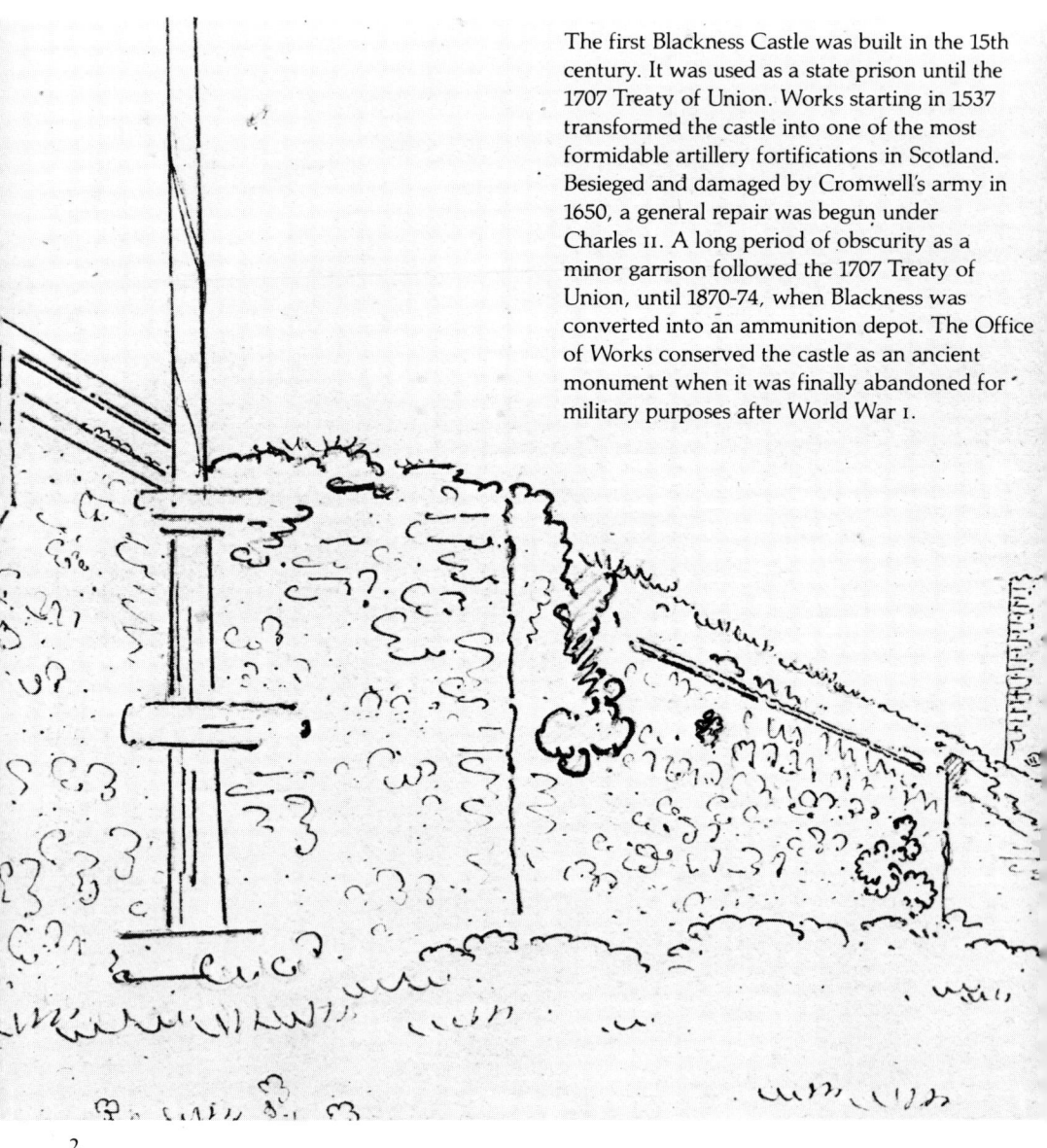

Inside the Castle courtyard, 1782.

History

Harbour, Castle and Prison

Castle of the Crichtons

The little cove of Blackness is the best natural harbour on the south side of the Firth of Forth west of Queensferry. In the middle ages it was the only feasible position for a seaport to serve the royal burgh of Linlithgow, about four miles inland. Ships are first mentioned as loading and unloading at Blackness in the year 1200, and the importance of Blackness increased with the choice of Linlithgow as a principal residence of the Kings of Scots. A castle at Blackness is not, however, mentioned until 1449. The evidence suggests that the first castle at Blackness was built, on the site of the castle that exists today, in the 1440s. By then the barony had passed through several ownerships into the possession of the Crichtons, one of the most powerful Scottish families. The first castle seems to have been built by Sir George Crichton, brother of the Chancellor of Scotland.

From the beginning the plan of Blackness Castle was dictated by the site, a long narrow spit of rock jutting into the Forth. Through the whole of the Castle's history until the 19th century, the rock spit was closely surrounded on three sides by sea or salt marsh. In the first building of the 1440s the site was cut off by a rock-cut ditch on the landward side to the south, and enclosed by a defensible wall with a blunt polygonal front towards the south,

Blackness Castle from the air, looking north over the Forth.

tapering northward to a point at the tip of the rocky spit. The wall was not particularly massive, and of modest height, topped by a simple parapet with crenellations—apertures spaced at intervals to allow the discharge of arrows and other missiles. The tower in the middle of the courtyard was probably built at the same time, together with residential accommodation against the walls, including a hall on the south side. The first historical mention of the castle in 1449 records its use as a state prison, a function which was to continue over two and a half centuries.

The castle in Royal hands

Blackness became a Royal castle in 1453, a gift by George Crichton to King James II, and it has been Crown property ever since. The castle was put in the charge of a captain or keeper, who was often also Sheriff of Linlithgow. Its use as state prison went on, for the most part holding men of middle or high rank. The best known prisoner of Blackness was Cardinal Beaton, who was confined there for about a month in 1543.

In 1543 a building-campaign had just been completed which transformed Blackness into one of the most formidable strongholds in Scotland, giving it much of the appearance it still has today. Sir James Hamilton of Finnart, in charge of royal works at Blackness and Linlithgow Palace, and also Keeper of Blackness, was given funds to begin works at Blackness Castle in 1537. Finnart, a bastard son of the first Earl of Arran, was a remarkable Renaissance Scot: at the same time a man of violence and a man of culture, knowledgeable in matters of architecture and military engineering. Finnart's own castle at Craignethan in Lanarkshire of the 1530s shows remarkable innovations in concepts of defence. The remodelled Blackness kept to the old plan, with enormously thickened walls on its most exposed front and incorporating generous provision for defensive guns.

The strengthened Blackness is of great interest in the story of the development of fortification to take account of artillery. It had none of the subtlety of the elaborate systems worked out in Italy, which were just beginning to penetrate to the rest of Europe: at Blackness a great brute mass of masonry confronted bombardment, with defensive guns positioned to give all-round firepower. Similar ideas of

defence had first appeared in Scotland at the blockhouse of Dunbar Castle, completed for the Regent of Scotland some 20 years earlier, and then at Tantallon Castle in a scheme of strengthening undertaken at the same time as these new works at Blackness.

Modifications seem to have gone on to the 1560s, in the reign of James V's daughter, Mary Queen of Scots. Blackness held out in support of Mary from the time of her abdication in 1567 until 1573, with the garrison harrying ships in the Forth and raiding the opposite shores of Fife. The castle was eventually blockaded but not formally besieged, and was in the end captured by a trick.

Siege did not come until 1650, during the conquest of Scotland by Oliver Cromwell's army. The place was bombarded by land and sea, with most damage being done by a battery emplaced on the high ground to the south. When the castle surrendered it was left in ruin by the English, and was not restored until the late 1660s.

The castle after 1707

After the Act of Union of 1707, which brought England and Scotland together as a United Kingdom, Blackness went out of use as a prison but was kept in repair, with a small garrison. In 1795 there were two gunners, a sergeant, two corporals and about a dozen privates: the posts of governor and deputy governor were held by non-resident officers as virtually honorary titles. The place had no real military value and the garrison dwindled until 1870–4, when the final phase of the castle's active life began as the central ammunition depot for Scotland. The War Office altered the superstructure of the towers, covered in the whole courtyard with an iron and cement roof, levelled an area east of the castle as a site for ammunition magazines, built new barracks with other garrison accommodation, and constructed a cast-iron pier out into the Forth from the castle. The regiment stationed in Edinburgh Castle provided a garrison for the depot, which fell out of use after less than forty years. In 1912 the castle was handed over to the Office of Works as an ancient monument. It was reoccupied during

It was during the reign of James V (above) that Blackness Castle was considerably modified: the development of siege artillery by the 16th century meant the need for a sound defensive stronghold was of utmost importance. As a result the walls of the castle were heightened and thickened and were pierced by numerous gunholes from which cannon and hand guns could be employed to keep would-be attackers at bay. By the end of James V's reign in 1542 Blackness had been converted from a baronial castle to a high profile artillery fort. (In the collection of the Scottish National Portrait Gallery: reproduced by kind permission of the National Galleries of Scotland.)

World War I and then finally abandoned. The Office of Works carried out a major programme of conservation and repair between 1926 and 1935. Save for the barracks, the pier and its drawbridge, the buildings erected after 1870 were demolished and the upper parts of the towers rebuilt to a resemblance of their ancient form.

A reconstruction drawing of the castle as it may have appeared in the 15th century. The original entrance gateway can be seen in the centre of the east wall.

Blackness Castle river-front from the north: a photograph circa 1920-30, showing the jetty in working order.

The South Tower: the patch of whitish stone shows the repair of major damage caused by the 1650 siege.

A Great Brute Mass of Masonry

Outside the castle

The surroundings of the castle only took on their present appearance in 1870–74 with the conversion and extension of Blackness as the central ammunition depot for Scotland. The shore to the east was reclaimed for now-demolished buildings and the rock-cut ditch in front of the south tower filled in. The reclaimed ground is now laid out as a lawn. Of other buildings constructed for the personnel of the depot, there survive the plain barrack block beneath the high ground to the south, and the Baronial style officers' quarters to the west.

South tower

To one standing beyond the south front of the castle, the main stages of its unusual development may be seen. As originally built in the 1440s, the wall at this south end rose to only half its present height. Its original parapet, overbuilt with later masonry, is emphasised in the drawing above.

In the works begun in 1537 this south front was massively thickened, raised in height and pierced by yawning oval-mouthed gunholes for defensive artillery, mounted in vaulted emplacements within. A cannon may have been mounted at the position of the big window—which seems originally to have been another gunhole—half-way up the tower. There were more guns behind the parapet. The east wall (right of drawing) was thickened, and a spur built jutting out to the west, as further improvements extending into the reign of Mary Queen of Scots (1542–67).

Drawing of the South Tower, emphasising the "fossilised" 15th century parapet.

The 16th century spur.

Blackness was besieged by Oliver Cromwell's generals in 1650 and badly damaged by gunfire before its surrender. Repairs carried out in 1667, using mostly whitish stone, show the extent of the damage. The largest patch partly obliterates one of the gunholes, by then disused.

The present parapet is a rebuilding of 1930-33, replacing a Victorian pitched roof, during the consolidation of the castle as an ancient monument.

East wall
The spacious entrance gateway of the 15th century castle pierced the east wall. It was blocked up as part of the strengthening of the castle after 1537 as an artillery fortress, when this wall was pierced by large gunholes. The blocking of the original entrance was removed by the Office of Works.

Spur
The 16th century spur jutting out to the west was originally approached by a drawbridge over a rock-cut ditch, now filled in. The spur had two functions, to provide a new heavily defended entrance replacing the vulnerable east gate, and to provide a wing battery to supplement the firepower of the south tower. The spur was altered and raised in height in 1693, when the round turret and the large square embrasures on each side of it were built.

Inside the castle
Enter the castle by the round-headed door in the spur with its 1693 wrought-iron yett or gate. The area within the spur was much reduced in size in 1693 by underbuilding for the upper gun platforms. The main courtyard of the castle is entered by a door to the right.

Courtyard
There were probably lean-to buildings around the courtyard from the beginning. All remains of these buildings save the foundations of the guard-house were removed when the Victorian ammunition depot was established and the

The Victorian drawbridge leading to the jetty.

courtyard spanned by a concrete and iron roof for use as a storehouse. The Victorian insertions in the courtyard were removed by the Office of Works after World War I. Near the entry to the courtyard from the spur, the gate and drawbridge leading out from the depot to a loading pier survive. The drawbridge is one of the last of its kind constructed in Britain.

Central tower

The Prison Tower, probably constructed as an original part of the first castle a few years before 1449, rises in the middle of the courtyard. Its chief use from an early date appears to have been to hold state prisoners, and other parts of the castle were probably used for the same purpose. It was raised in height and its security improved as part of the building campaign of 1537–42, and it was again altered in 1667 when the projecting stair-tower was built. After use as a prison ended in 1707 the tower was converted into a barracks. Restoration was carried out by the Office of Works in 1931–34.

The original tower had three storeys and an attic above a vaulted basement. When altered

In the earliest castle the principal residential unit, a hall and chamber raised on basements, was built against the back of the low defensive wall. A flight of steps led up to the hall.

In 1537–42 the outer wall was pierced by five large gunholes, the wall itself was massively reinforced to give a maximum thickness of 5.5 metres, the lower part was vaulted and the whole structure raised to its present height to form the south tower. The gunholes were of the largest size found in Scotland at that date, apparently meant for guns mounted on carriages. The work is one of the best examples in Scotland of early response to gunpowder weapons.

The work was further strengthened in two stages during the reign of Mary Queen of Scots (1542–67). First, three of the five internal gun emplacements were partly filled with masonry, reducing a possible source of weakness at the base of the wall.

Second, the spur was built out from the west side of the castle. A vaulted gallery, reached by a narrow tunnel from the south tower (and unfortunately too awkward for access by visitors) was loopholed for small handguns to cover the approach to the gate and the interior of the spur.

The central tower seen from the eastern rampart.

between 1537 and 1542 a vault was built over the third storey eliminating the attic. The walls of the tower were raised, building up from the old parapet which, like the parapet of the south tower, may be seen 'fossilized' in the later work. The heightened tower was given a new ornate parapet which could accommodate artillery.

Internally, the three rooms above the basement are spacious, with a fireplace and a garderobe or latrine; two of the three rooms have closets opening off them. It is apparent that this was no ordinary Scottish gaol: many of its inmates, mostly political prisoners, were men of rank and consequence and had some degree of comfort in confinement.

South tower

Leave the Prison Tower to approach the south tower, introduced in describing the exterior. Its development is shown in the following cutaway drawings.

Interior view showing the South Tower seated on natural rock.

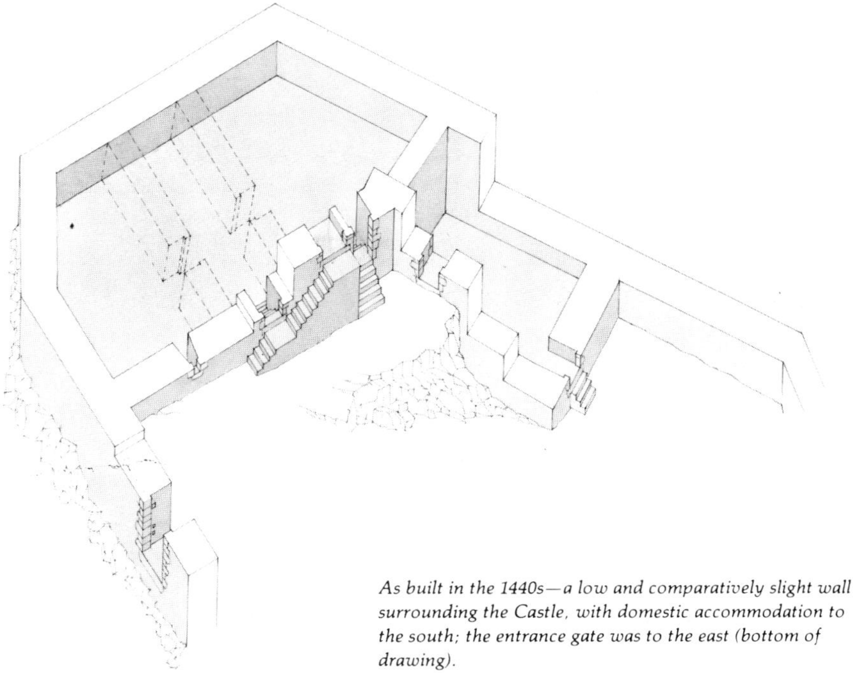

As built in the 1440s—a low and comparatively slight wall surrounding the Castle, with domestic accommodation to the south; the entrance gate was to the east (bottom of drawing).

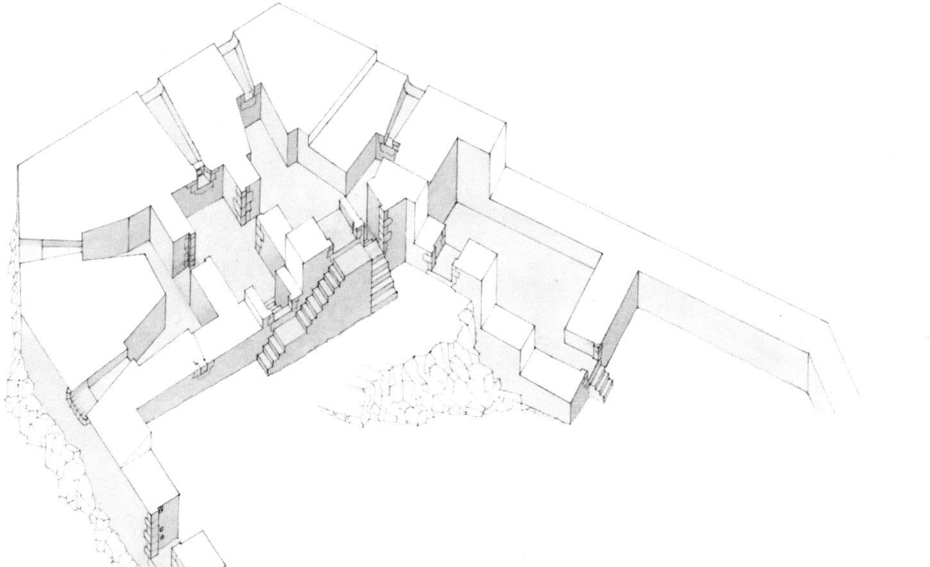

First stage of improvement as artillery fortification, 1537-42, in the reign of James V. Walls massively thickened and pierced by gun-holes; the whole of the southern part raised at the same time to form the present South Tower.

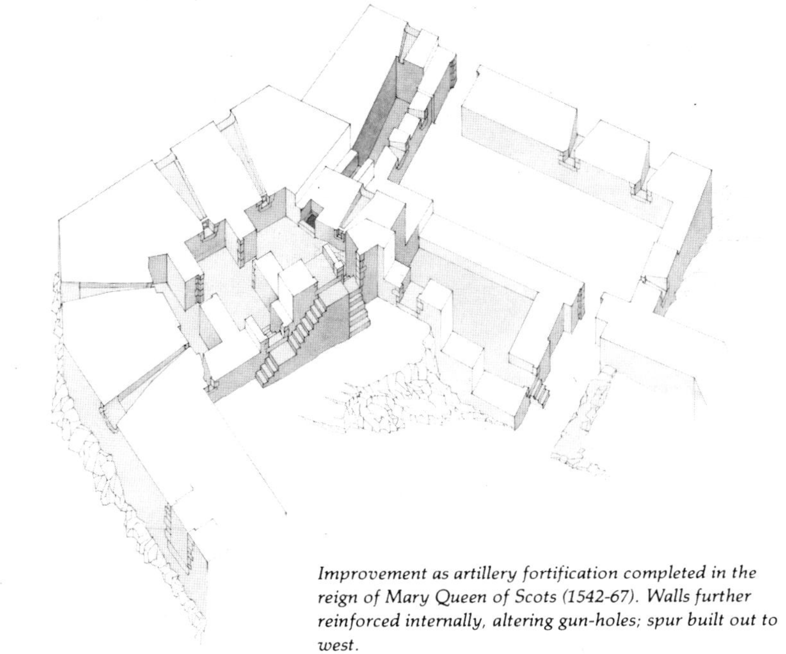

Improvement as artillery fortification completed in the reign of Mary Queen of Scots (1542-67). Walls further reinforced internally, altering gun-holes; spur built out to west.

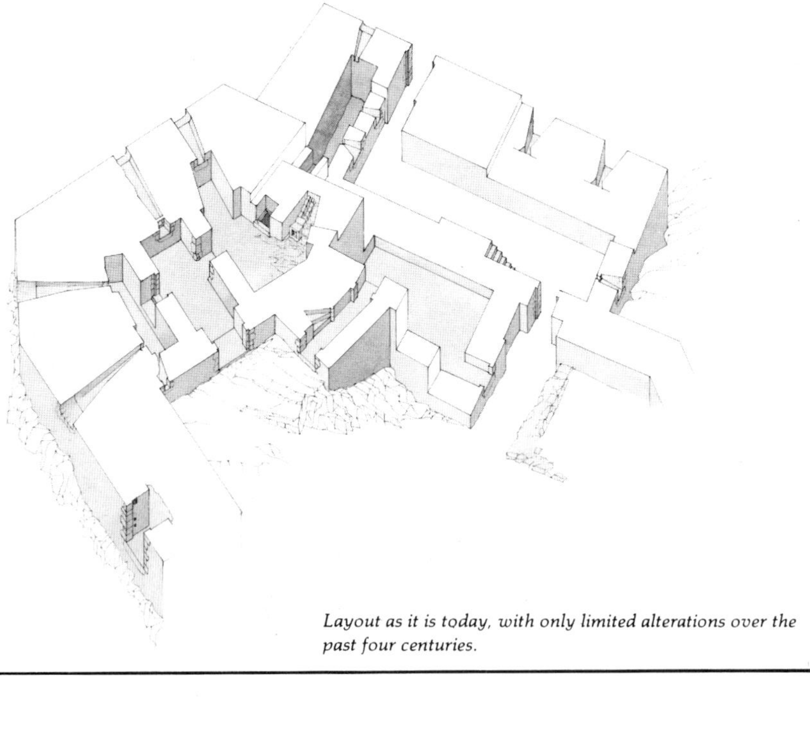

Layout as it is today, with only limited alterations over the past four centuries.

Building operations at the south tower begun in 1677 were chiefly required to make good the damage caused by the 1650 Cromwellian siege. At the same time the ground-level gun emplacements were abandoned and blocked while part of this level was converted into the castle bakehouse. (The ovens were removed and the gunholes opened out in 1926–35.)

These lower parts of the South Tower are today not much different from the arrangements at the end of Mary's reign. Leaving the emplacements, a stair, also of 1667, between the main block of the tower and its wing, gives access to the upper floors. They largely retain the basic planning of 1537–42 with alterations of 1667. In the principal room of the south tower, the hall, provision was still made in 1677 for a great gun to be mounted in its largest window in time of need, while the original height of the hall was reduced by the insertion of an extra floor. The suite of private rooms in the wing, opening from the hall, represents a complete replanning of 1667. Note the typically Scottish half-glazed and half-shuttered windows, replicas inserted by the Office of Works in the 1920s.

The stair continues up to the parapet. Almost all the detail here is restoration by the Office of Works. It is clear that when the whole south front was raised in 1537–42 it was intended to mount guns at this level to oppose any battery established on the high ground to the south.

Tour of wallheads

Returning to the foot of the stair, turn right and ascend the steps leading to the parapet of the east wall, greatly thickened along most of its length in the 16th century, and with a parapet restored by the Office of Works. The further end of the east wall, narrowing to its original width, gives access to the triangular north tower. Originally much higher, the latter was reduced and platforms provided for three guns in 1693.

The west wall was altered to its present width and height in 1667. Commanding superb views of the Firth of Forth, it leads to the upper gun platforms and now-roofless turret of the spur as remodelled in 1693. A stair descends to the courtyard of the spur, concluding the tour of what was in its day one of the strongest places in Scotland.

The castle from the east.

15

Interior view of the castle courtyard in the 1920s.

Further Reading

D MacGibbon and T Ross, *The Castellated and Domestic Architecture of Scotland*, volume 3 (Edinburgh 1889)

Royal Commission on Ancient and Historical Monuments of Scotland, *Inventory of Midlothian and West Lothian* (Edinburgh 1929)

Craignethan Castle, HMSO Guidebook (1978)

S H Cruden, *The Scottish Castle* (Edinburgh 1981)

Iain MacIvor, 'Artillery and Major Places of Strength in the Lothians and East Borders, 1513–1542' in (ed) David Caldwell *Scottish Weapons and Fortifications 1100–1800* (Edinburgh 1981)

C J Tabraham, *Scottish Castles and Fortifications* (Edinburgh 1986)

Tantallon Castle, HMSO Guidebook (1989)